PRODUCTS: FROM IDEA TO MARKET
Video Games

by Abby Doty

www.focusreaders.com

Copyright © 2025 by Focus Readers®, Mendota Heights, MN 55120. All rights reserved. No part of this book may be reproduced or utilized in any form or by any means without written permission from the publisher.

Focus Readers is distributed by North Star Editions:
sales@northstareditions.com | 888-417-0195

Produced for Focus Readers by Red Line Editorial.

Photographs ©: Shutterstock Images, cover, 1, 4, 6, 14, 22, 26; iStockphoto, 8, 11, 13, 17, 19, 21, 29; Jan Woitas/picture-alliance/dpa/AP Images, 25

Library of Congress Cataloging-in-Publication Data
Names: Doty, Abby, author.
Title: Video games: from idea to market / Abby Doty.
Description: Mendota Heights, MN: Focus Readers, 2025. | Series: Products: from idea to market | Includes index. | Audience: Grades 2-3 |
Identifiers: LCCN 2024025132 (print) | LCCN 2024025133 (ebook) | ISBN 9798889984092 (hardcover) | ISBN 9798889984375 (paperback) | ISBN 9798889984900 (pdf) | ISBN 9798889984658 (ebook)
Subjects: LCSH: Video games--Design--Juvenile literature. | Video games--Marketing--Juvenile literature.
Classification: LCC GV1469.3 .D68 2025 (print) | LCC GV1469.3 (ebook) | DDC 794.8--dc23/eng/20240607
LC record available at https://lccn.loc.gov/2024025132
LC ebook record available at https://lccn.loc.gov/2024025133

Printed in the United States of America
Mankato, MN
012025

About the Author

Abby Doty is a writer, editor, and booklover from Minnesota.

Table of Contents

CHAPTER 1

New Fighter Game 5

CHAPTER 2

Video Game Design 9

CHAPTER 3

Making a Game 15

THAT'S AMAZING!

Virtual Reality 20

CHAPTER 4

Video Game Ads 23

Focus Questions • 28

Glossary • 30

To Learn More • 31

Index • 32

CHAPTER 1

New Fighter Game

A girl rushes into her living room. She has a new fighting video game. She got the game for her birthday. The girl puts the game in her **console**. Then she grabs a controller. She sits down to play.

Video game controllers have buttons. People push them to take different actions in the game.

Some gamers use equipment such as headsets. But many games can be played without them.

The game's images look bright and clear. The characters move smoothly. The girl loves the game's music, too. She invites her friend to play. Her friend joins the game online. The girls laugh and talk while they play.

Their characters jump across the screen. They fight enemies. Every part of the game is fun. Both girls love it. They wonder how someone created the game.

Did You Know?

Some online video games are multiplayer games. People far apart can use the internet to play together.

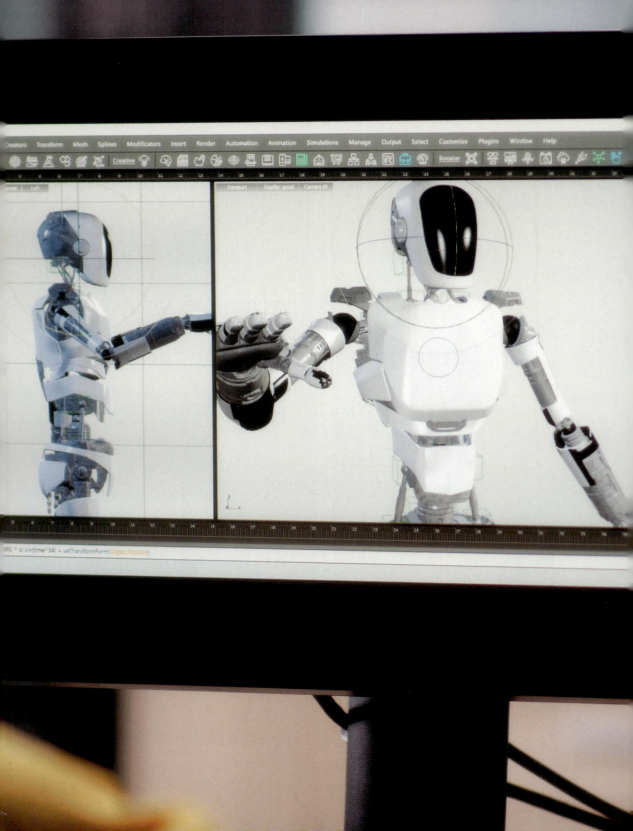

CHAPTER 2

Video Game Design

Developers create new video games. First, developers come up with new ideas. They need **inspiration**. Developers can find inspiration in many ways. They may notice things around them.

Developers' ideas may start with an interesting character.

9

Often, developers play other video games. They see which parts work well. Developers look at gamers' reactions, too. They learn how people feel about those games. Developers use all this information. Their ideas get stronger.

Next, developers start planning. They choose the **genre** of their game. They figure out the game's storyline. They come up with the characters and settings, too. And they choose the game's format. For

Video games have many different genres. They include sports, puzzle, and horror games.

example, they decide if it should be single player or multiplayer. All these decisions are important. They affect how the team designs the game.

11

After that, the team makes early **prototypes**. Prototypes can include playable parts of the game. People try them out. These tests help developers find out what works.

Prototypes include art, too. Drawings show how the game will look. Artists may sketch out

Did You Know?

Pong came out in 1972. In the game, players hit a ball back and forth. *Pong* helped make video games popular.

Artists try to make the game's visuals unique and exciting.

the plot. For example, they use storyboards to show each scene. Then other people offer feedback to designers. Developers keep working until the design is just right.

CHAPTER 3
Making a Game

Once the designs are ready, game companies start making the full games. Teams include many people. They all do different jobs. Developers, writers, artists, and voice actors all help.

 Animators make characters move.

Developers bring their prototype to life. They build the characters and levels of the game. They design details such as lighting and game menus. To do that, developers write lots of **code**. This code tells computer **software** how to run the game. Many developers use game

Did You Know?

Small game companies may have just a few workers. Large companies may have hundreds.

> Making a video game is expensive. Big games can cost more than $100 million to create.

engines. The engines have some pre-made code that developers can use. These programs help people create games more quickly.

Other workers add their parts, too. Artists finalize the game's look.

Voice actors record the characters' words. Then, teams put everything together. Ideas often change during this process. Parts from the prototype might not work. But eventually, the teams create a finished game.

Then, people in the company try the game. They look for mistakes. They fix any problems. The teams make sure everything works.

When a game is done, it is time to sell it. Some games are online.

 If a game has sequels, the same voice actors might return to voice their parts again.

Customers download the games or connect online. Other times, people play on consoles. They use physical items. Often, games come on glass discs. Companies use machines to etch games onto the discs. Then consoles read the discs.

THAT'S AMAZING!

Virtual Reality

The first **virtual reality** (VR) headset came out in the 1960s. Players could see a room. The room had a few simple items. The first headset was heavy and slow. But soon, people created new ones. They were faster and better.

In the 2010s, many companies created VR video games. New technology helped track movement. Some pieces tracked a player's eyes. Others tracked their body and hands. Then the player's character moved inside the game.

By the 2020s, VR games cost less. The technology became even more popular.

 VR headsets can be useful for training. People can practice difficult tasks without any risk.

CHAPTER 4
Video Game Ads

Companies want buyers to choose their games. So, they **advertise** in different ways. Many companies make trailers. These videos tell customers what a game is about. They can show what it looks like.

Ads might tell customers what age a game is made for.

Trailers usually come out before the game does. That builds excitement. Customers may want to buy the game right away.

Many video games are played online. Companies often make online ads. Gamers can see them on game websites. Companies may even create online communities. Workers can use social media to talk to gamers.

In addition, some gamers show their gameplay online. Game

Some video game streamers have millions of viewers.

companies may pay these people to play their games. That way, more people will see those games.

Often, companies keep improving their games. They make changes even after the games come out.

Some people play games at cyber cafes. Companies can host events there.

Sometimes companies fix mistakes. Other times, they add something. For example, developers might include new levels. Then companies advertise the new editions. Bonus content can keep players interested for a long time.

26

Video game conventions also connect companies and gamers. Players, developers, and company workers all go to them. Companies can show off their new products. And gamers can find new games they will love.

Did You Know?

Gamescom in Germany is the world's largest gaming convention. More than 1,000 companies show their games there.

Focus Questions

Write your answers on a separate piece of paper.

1. Write a few sentences explaining the main ideas of Chapter 3.

2. Would you like to create video games? Why or why not?

3. What is one way that people come up with new video game ideas?
   - **A.** People create video game discs.
   - **B.** People play other video games.
   - **C.** People fix video game mistakes.

4. Why might companies want to talk to gamers online?
   - **A.** so companies can write more code with gamers
   - **B.** so companies hear fewer opinions from gamers
   - **C.** so companies can get more gamers interested in their games

5. What does **storyboards** mean in this book?

*Drawings show how the game will look. Artists may sketch out the plot. For example, they use **storyboards** to show each scene.*

    A. a set of images
    B. a long book
    C. a game's music

6. What does **eventually** mean in this book?

*Ideas often change during this process. Parts from the prototype might not work. But **eventually**, the teams create a finished game.*

    A. right away
    B. later on
    C. before anything else

Answer key on page 32.

Glossary

advertise
To make messages or videos about a product so customers want to buy it.

code
Instructions that tell a computer or device what to do.

console
A computer system made specifically for video games.

developers
People who make and design video games.

genre
A type or category of something.

inspiration
Something that gives a person ideas.

prototypes
Original forms of something, usually for testing.

software
The programs that run on a computer and perform certain functions.

virtual reality
An artificial world that a person can interact with.

To Learn More

BOOKS

Bolte, Mari. *Super Surprising Trivia About Video Games*. North Mankato, MN: Capstone Press, 2024.

Gish, Ashley. *MOBA Games*. Mendota Heights, MN: Apex Editions, 2024.

Rathburn, Betsy. *Video Game Developer*. Minneapolis: Bellwether Media, 2023.

NOTE TO EDUCATORS

Visit **www.focusreaders.com** to find lesson plans, activities, links, and other resources related to this title.

Index

A
advertising, 23, 26
artists, 13, 15, 17

C
characters, 6–7, 10, 16, 18, 20
code, 16–17
consoles, 5, 19
conventions, 27

D
designs, 11, 13, 15–16
developers, 9–10, 12–13, 15–17, 26–27
discs, 19

G
game engines, 16–17
genres, 10

I
inspiration, 9–10

M
multiplayer games, 7, 11

O
online, 7, 18–19, 24

P
prototypes, 12, 16, 18

S
single player games, 11
software, 16

T
technology, 20
trailers, 23–24

V
virtual reality, 20
voice actors, 15, 18